The World As It Is

John Taylor

The World As It Is

John Taylor

Cedar Hill Publications

3722 Hwy. 8 West
Mena, AR 71953
(501) 394-7029

Senior Editor: *Christopher Presfield*
Managing Editor: *Gloria Doyle*

ACKNOWLEDGEMENTS

The author would like to thank the following reviews, in which many of the texts from the first section, *The Voyage to Tenderness,* first appeared: *Cedar Hill Review, Expressive Spirals, George & Mertie's Place: Rooms with a View, The Glass Cherry, Horizon* (Belgium), *Intuitive Explorations, Paper Boat, The Pegasus Review, Red Owl Magazine, The Tennessee Quarterly, 360 Degrees.*

The review *Kestrel* published six of these texts, as well as a preface, under the title *Six Apperceptions.* The first text of *The Voyage to Tenderness* was published as a bilingual broadside at the Festival de la Nouvelle, in Saint-Quentin, France, in 1995. It was entitled "Our Mysterious Island."

The title of this first series of apperceptions, *The Voyage to Tenderness,* is derived from the French salon game "la carte de Tendre" (as invented by the 17th-century writer Mlle de Scudéry). It was a game devoted to "love's progress" and involved a "country" or a "realm" of Tendre (the old French word for Tenderness). One "voyaged" on the map of Tenderness.

Some of the texts grouped here under the title *Seven Apperceptions* were first published in *American Writing, Tight,* and *World Letter.* "Autumnal" was first published, in French, in the review *Harfang* (Angers), in a special issue devoted to contemporary writing from the Lower Loire Valley.

The story *Into the Waves* was originally commissioned by the French small-press publisher Isoète (Cherbourg). It appeared, in French, under the title *Au cœur des vagues* (1994), in a translation by Françoise Daviet. It was first published in English in *Pangolin Papers* (Winter 1997).

The epigraph is taken from Jean-Philippe Salabreuil's "Commentaire." This text was first published by Claude Michel Cluny in his edition of Salabreuil's *La Liberté des feuilles* (La Différence, Collection "Orphée," 1990).

The cover is by the French artist Sibylle Baltzer-Hasan.

The Voyage to Tenderness 7

Seven Apperceptions 45

Into the Waves. 57

This book is for Nature and for Justin

The Voyage to Tenderness

We walked often along that river which, not too long afterwards, was dammed up, turned into a lake.

The trail rose over oak roots, skirted clumps of poison ivy; here and there it disappeared into puddles; only in rare stretches was it wide enough for two.

You would say: *I enjoy a harmony here I can't find elsewhere.*

The trail eventually climbed to an asphalt road leading out of the woods. Cars would be parked there, families picnicking in the clearing. We would head back.

Most of the trail followed the edge of the river bank, several feet above the water. But there was one place— remember?—where the path dipped to a narrow beach.

It was usually on our way back that we lingered there.

Right in front of us, as we gazed over the slow-moving, brownish water, lay a sandbar covered with thick bushes. From their midst rose a tall, leafless, sun-bleached tree. We called the sandbar *our mysterious island.*

One afternoon you tried to convince me that a human face, hidden in the bushes, was staring at us. I almost believed you. I wanted to believe you. That afternoon ended strangely: we laughed about the face, then hugged each other—for the first and last time.

One autumn day—it was the next-to-last-time we walked along the river—we stopped on the beach, opposite the mysterious island. You were talking. I was listening. Eventually you suggested we sit down, lean back against the cold, muddy bank. I pointed out how wet and dirty we would be. You said: *Oh, who cares?* I acquiesced, picked up a twig to keep in my hand, then sat down beside you, placing myself close enough so that, from time to time, I would feel the pressure of your elbow—through our thick wool jackets.

I drove to my favorite spot in the countryside.

Everything reminded me of you, of what I thought it was like where you lived—so far away.

The Canadian thistles along the road; the wild geese gliding downwards through the air; the cows grazing on the other side of the river.

I imagined that we were walking along the river, holding hands.

I imagined that we had few words to say, that our togetherness sufficed, that the slow-flowing river sufficed, that the sunset sufficed.

I imagined you with me—everything reminded me of you. The blades of grass. The goldfinch on the sandy bank.

I loved these natural things (as you would have loved them); then, gradually, they sufficed no more.

In my mind you slowly turned to face me. We were going to embrace. I contemplated your loveliness for an instant. . . .

Suddenly, you were no longer there.

I clung desperately to what remained of your presence—until, inexorably, you once again became an absence, set against the backdrop of the natural world.

I learned, through a chance conversation in a bar, that you were probably the other foreigner staying in that same small sea resort.

Then, a few days later, as I was walking up a steep street to fetch something from the car, I noticed a woman coming down a narrow path to the right. I waited. It was very early in the morning. No one else was about. When I looked closely: it was you.

You approached, then, having recognized me, stopped, remaining at a distance that suggested you were afraid.

Comment vas-tu? I asked in French, a language that, twenty years before, we had often pretended to speak, although we knew only a few words. Sometimes, in our hometown, we had stopped passersby and asked directions in broken English, as if we were lost tourists. *Que deviens-tu?*

You obviously understood nothing, so I chuckled:

You probably don't even know that I ended up living in France.

You looked at me with a certain neutrality, as if unsurprised; perhaps you were only indifferent.

You have of course aged, I thought, but, yes, here was the face I had cherished—still so surprisingly youthful, tanned, the skin somehow *tight.* (*...her skin tight and pale,* I had once written in a story.)

I remembered how we would play tennis together, you so ferociously. Although I didn't know how to serve correctly, if I concentrated I could nearly always win. So, once in a while, I only stabbed with my backhand.

A silence had fallen between us and, because you continued to say nothing, I wondered how—in what exact ways—you had changed. Before, you had never concealed your feelings, even momentarily. I recalled how you had once, while speeding down the interstate, pulled over into the emergency lane, stopped the car, and sobbed uncontrollably.

We should have a cup of coffee together, I suggested, indicating a bar up the street. There were chairs and tables outside; the sun was rising over the rooftops; the proprietor was opening up. Holding a dishtowel in his hand, he looked in our direction—curious, perhaps even wary.

You hesitated, shook your head—almost an unconscious twitch meaning _no._

You said:

Maybe, in a few days.

You know as well as I do, I replied, with a self-confidence that I never could have mustered back then, _that if we don't have our talk right now, we never will._

I won't bring up the past, I added. _I promise._

You seemed almost on the verge of agreeing when you vanished. Vanished!

In a moment everything vanished.

I was staring into the darkness of the bedroom. Noises of the early-morning traffic came through the shutters; then a bus rumbled down the rue Louis-Gain.

I lay in bed for quite some time, searching for the words of the dream. They seemed to be in my mind; but they also seemed to hover between my eyes and the ceiling. Whenever I located a few, I repeated them to myself. I added other words, making sentences.

Finally I got up, groped my way to the living room, turned on a lamp, wrote them down. It was six o'clock in the dead of winter. A neighbor turned on his electric coffee grinder.

After writing the words down, I went back to bed, but not to sleep.

I didn't think of too many of those desperate mo-
ments—from twenty years before—no, not too many of
them, but rather continued to call your face back to mind.
You kept vanishing, but I could call you back. I could
concentrate and look at you for a moment. My serenity
was almost complete—almost. I kept calling you back
before my eyes, my serenity almost complete, amazed
that we had run into each other—one last time, after all
that had happened, after all those years—in that quaint
little foreign town near the sea.

I dreamt that we were watching a film in a very dark cinema and that, wishing to tell me something, you touched the back of my left hand with your fingertips. Your fingertips stayed there and, gradually, your entire hand slipped into mine. We held hands until the end of the film—Bergman's *Wild Strawberries*. When the lights came on, we looked at each other benevolently, serenely. The hand-holding had strengthened something between us that had always—it was now evident—existed.

Before we stood up, however, I suddenly, desperately, confessed my love. It was a "teenager-like" confession (indeed resembling several I had actually made during my adolescence), and when I awoke I couldn't remember how you had reacted—if you had reacted at all. Perhaps the dream had simply ended. *So be it,* I sighed, in fact re-lieved. I got out of bed, went to the kitchen, made myself a cup of coffee.

Still, a morning went by, followed by nearly an entire afternoon, and I was tempted to copy the dream onto a postcard and send it to you.

How could I reword it slightly, I kept wondering (though doubting that I would actually follow through on my whim), so that you would merely laugh at having been dreamt about, after so many years and in a distant country, and not take my simple card as a belated, yet genuine, confession?

We were sitting side by side, on a stone parapet.

The others were moving away, you rose to follow, I restrained you gently by touching your arm.

You sat back down, and looked me in the eyes.

I said: *Let's find a place to have dinner, by ourselves.*

Yet this—all this—I have imagined.

Once, a long time ago, we sat on a stone parapet, before rising and joining the others.

*

Years had passed. It was a crisp, cloudless Sunday morning.

A black butterfly with orange-tipped wings alit on a board. I studied it.

A propeller plane passed overhead.

Leaves of a sycamore—strangely—trembled.

Warm sunlight, on the back of my hand.

I wondered: The three beauty spots—did you also recall them from time to time?

*

You visited me in a dream one night, but I can't remember what you did, what you said.

At the end, you were standing in the entryway.

I touched your hair, I caressed the top of your head, I kissed you.

But we could no longer linger there—you were leaving.

Did you leave?

Did I cry afterwards?

Just before waking, I was hurrying back to the entryway, bearing a message.

*

It was hard to admit that, were we together, all would once again be destroyed. And I couldn't help but imagine an encounter, coincidental, unexpected—a freeway rest area, a hotel in an out-of-the-way place, a busy street in a metropolis. Or, simply, anywhere. Chance itself would seal our fate. Yet what was our fate? I knew—too well. I persisted, imagining other outcomes. I took your hand in my hand. We turned and walked away. Away. Away. Away. Yet, in the end, as before, my doubts and your bitterness.

You were almost never home.

Sometimes I took walks in the evening, called you from a telephone booth.

The phone would ring, unanswered.

I would walk blocks and blocks, sit in the park, once or twice stop to talk to a friend. Then I would try again.

The phone would ring; my stacks of quarters ready.

The phone would ring.

Oh yes, one evening you answered. And another evening.

Days, sometimes weeks, went by in the meantime. I wrote you letters; my stacks of quarters rose. In your postcards you apologized for not being home more often.

Is there someone else in your life? I asked one evening, a tremor in my voice.

You answered:

No.

You went on about a subject that concerned neither of us at first hand—an election, a war, hunger in the world, whatever.

I kept putting my quarters into the slot; clicks, through your words, as the coins fell.

I saved every quarter, thinking of you. Sometimes I resolved never to call you again. Then I would go out for a walk, passing by telephone booths, always entering one at the end. I would put in several quarters, listen to the phone ring.

Ring.

Ring.

When I hung up, the coins would fall through the phone, with a clatter.

Your face like a guardian angel's. The months that went by—three, exactly—during which I nursed, in you, wounds of a love lost elsewhere.

I would walk you home (you would ask to leave), the sidewalks covered with snow so high we followed tire tracks in the street.

The tracks kept us apart: suddenly, a more comfortable distance.

I would point out how beautiful the silence was, how the snowflakes fell softly through the yellow cones of light.

Don't you want to turn back?

One night, I asked you this question.

And you replied:

Imagine the certitude of having no more emotions at all. Just the snow falling everywhere and forever.

We met, three years later, in the reception room of a hotel.

You were pregnant. Your silhouette revealed: six months, seven months. When I asked, you replied: *In April*.

As if nothing had evolved between us, I first expected a gaiety, an effervescence, to emanate from our encounter; but, almost as soon, I felt ill at ease, and both of us searched for things to say.

In a moment I asked: *The boyfriend you told me about?*

You looked downward, shook your head; I regretted my indiscretion.

Still, I persisted: *Do you want a boy? A girl?*

Others joined us. Glasses of wine were passed around; you laughed, as you always did when offered a drink, then said you wouldn't have one.

The baby, you smiled, gently stroking your round stomach. Deborah offered grandmotherly advice. Susan, who knew you only a little, took your arm and said: *It's marvelous*. I couldn't help but recall, once again in regard to that remote boyfriend, that we had drunk too much together, one evening, now seemingly ages ago.

After the toastings I had to leave.

I desired to kiss you tenderly on the cheek, and did. Then I gave your arm a squeeze, and asked: *Will you let me know when your child is born?*

You promised you would, but, when I left the hotel and hurried down the alleyway, having refused the ride that George had offered me although I was wondering whether I would make it to the taxi stand, then to the airport, on time, I couldn't understand what your eyes had expressed more than once: Were they bidding me good-bye forever? Were they telling me of some unfathomable pain?

We had been traveling in Europe for several weeks, leaving each morning for a new destination. I was not sure which end-of-the-century it was. Although, true to form, I remained skeptical of all replies, I occasionally asked strangers or other travelers to tell me the year. Most of them answered: '95.

The weather was balmy, unchanging, even on the Baltic in winter. Little motion was in fact perceptible in our midst, the entire world having become scenery for our *rapprochement*. This word was, strangely—or perhaps appropriately—our talisman, and we both pronounced it several times a day.

Contrary to your habits, you were wearing silk night-gowns and ankle-length dresses during the various episodes of this trip, which from most appearances was a sort of honeymoon. In the afternoons, we made love for hours, tender caresses evolving into passionate penetrations. In the evenings, we dined in vast chandeliered restaurants. I would rest my fingertips on your forearm while we were waiting for delicacies, gaze into your eyes while you talked about the immediate past or the immediate future.

How had our original departure come about?

I could no longer remember (or perhaps did not know), and this unanswered question from time to time worried me (*slightly,* I kept reassuring myself).

Just before waking I realized I was dreaming and the awareness of approaching a border like none we had ever crossed made me, I suppose, open my eyes—with apprehension.

Immediately I closed them, attempted to redream. Scenes set in hotel suites or on ocean boardwalks were repeated, rehearsed, once again. I wondered if anything of what we were experiencing together was being recuperated for the undreamt present—*that is,* I corrected myself, *for the undreamt future that will become a present, my present, our present.*

Accompanying these cogitations was a nocturne by Field. We were the only couple dancing in the ballroom; no, we were not really dancing, but rather—in the center of the floor—simply standing there, holding on to each other. I whispered into your ear—*Listen*—and the tuxedoed pianist lifted his hands from the keyboard.

You were wearing blue tennis shoes, just like those I had worn myself, so many years before.

Then (so many years before), after my blue tennis shoes had worn out, after my parents had thrown them away, we couldn't find a new pair anywhere. We looked in shops all over town. I don't really know why, it seemed something tragic had happened: as if my blue tennis shoes had not worn out, but been lost. As if they were irreplaceable, a vital part of my very being. *So what?* I said to myself over and again. Words didn't help. For weeks, months, I couldn't get over that pair of blue tennis shoes. I had felt good—comfortable—at home—myself—in them.

After a while, I thought about them less and less, then forgot them completely.

When we sat on the edge of the fountain to talk and I looked down at your feet, everything came back in a flush of sadness: the loss. I didn't tell you everything I felt. I couldn't.

All I said was:

I like your blue tennis shoes.

You seemed surprised. Had I ever complimented you on your clothing? Surely not. You looked at me inquisitively. Your eyes said:

This is not really you.

Which was true: I was not really myself.

Or rather: I was all too much myself.

You laughed, with a twinge of nervousness.

Oh, I bought them for next to nothing, in a supermarket. They're Chinese.

I nodded.

Of course.

I told you about my similar pair—when I was a kid.

Then I said:

One day they wore out and my parents couldn't find a new pair anywhere. It was strange. I became very sad. For a while, I even thought I would never get over it.

You looked at me, tenderly, understandingly, but also with a slight exasperation, as if you had concluded I was once again speaking allusively or in parables.

I looked down at your feet again—or perhaps at mine—or at nothing at all—, then back up into your eyes.

A silence fell between us.

I waited for you all day long, on the hunch that you would be passing through. That is, I waited for you at my hometown train station, which, miraculously, had continued to function despite the disappearance of the train system. I met every Rock Island from the first (7:14 a.m.) to the last (9:04 p.m.). Tears streamed from my eyes every time I had to admit—as still another train pulled away from the station—that you had not only not gotten off, run towards me, hugged me, but indeed that we had not even been able to wave at each other during the two-minute stop. The tinted window panes of the passenger cars were so dark I could hardly make out any faces inside. Yet I sought yours desperately, running from car to car, from window to window, pressing my nose against the glass. Between trains I paced up and down the platform, contemplating ways of ending my life. Towards evening a policeman began watching me and, after the last train had departed for Minneapolis (leaving me devastated), he led me away. I let him handcuff me. It mattered little. I had retreated into my loneliness, wondering whether we were destined to ever meet again.

Ushered into the asylum, I awoke.

Later that day I had to pick up some reservations—at the train station in the French town where I now live. After signing my check, pushing it underneath the window and receiving my tickets, I strolled out onto the platform, lingered there for a while, not really expecting you of course, but knowing I would continue to ponder these strange sentiments I had felt for you, in a dream.

Lying in bed, unable to sleep, I imagined myself getting up, standing at the window, waiting for a lone car to rush down the street below.

And when that car finally appeared (on the street below, as I was listening), pulled up at the light, stopped, waited, accelerated, sped past, disappeared behind the building, I remembered (in a dream, having by now dozed off) how we had once driven onto the freeway, nearly twenty-five years before, after that play at the Community Playhouse.

We were seventeen years old; life seemed formed of possibilities. Always more adventurous, you said: *I have twenty dollars in my purse.*

We made plans, laughed about our plans, later grew silent.

We sped eastward, through the darkness.

We sped past imaginable vistas of frozen cornfields— become invisible.

You put your head on my shoulder; you fingered, just above my right knee, the crease in my black woolen pants. Your silence was like a sigh.

Time (I realized) was going by. But I tried to cherish those moments, every moment. And in the dream I tried to cherish them *even more desperately.*

Even more desperately—those exact words I repeated to myself, now aware that I was waking.

Inexplicable disks and dashes of light—on the dashboard, on the bedroom walls. I struggled to imagine our driving onward, guided by similar lights. The buzz of an alarm clock. Cars on the street below. I turned on the bedside lamp. Night had come to an end.

I kissed you and was punished—by Miss Hamilton.

Twelve years later you turned up in my high school.

You had been thrown out of several high schools by then.

For a few weeks you sat in my classes—a treacherous beauty.

Once or twice we talked—you remembered me. You even confessed a secret.

Then you disappeared forever.

I never told anyone your secret.

This morning, while walking across a public garden, I suddenly remembered you.

I remembered your terrible secret.

The air was cold and crisp. The sky had not yet lost its rose tinge from the dawn. Workers were planting flowers around a new statue.

I remembered you and your name, you were a little girl with brown hair and freckles on your cheeks, you were sitting next to me in that reading circle that we formed.

Miss Hamilton was saying something.

I stood up, turned, bent down, and kissed your lips.

After working last night—past midnight—, I suddenly wondered what you might be doing, whether I could call you.

But how to call you, twenty-four years ago?

Do you remember? Snow flurries, icy streets; by eight o'clock everyone inside; curtains drawn, afghans out, televisions on. A friend of ours was throwing a Christmas party. We decided to go together, neither of us having anyone else at the moment.

That is, we were the closest of friends—and a little more than that.

You knew lots of poetry by heart; your eyes were dark brown; we had known each other since childhood. The street you lived on was the only cobblestone one left in the city.

Do you remember? A latecomer announced: *Your front tire's flat!* Several of us pushed my car onto the steep driveway. Our friend's father changed that tire all by himself; it was eight degrees below zero. *Enjoy life while you can!* he joked, then waved us back into the party.

When we parted that night we hesitated, then kissed each other on the lips—more tenderly than if we had been lovers.

And the next morning, when I awoke, I wondered: *Are you the one?*

You were not. But we tried. And that tenderness that we had experienced crumbled away.

*

Last night—past midnight—, suddenly remembering you, I looked over my books. You admired Wallace Stevens and I opened a selection of his poems.

> *God and all angels sing the world to sleep*
> *Now that the moon is rising in the heat*

And crickets are loud again in the grass. The moon
Burns in the mind on lost remembrances . . . .

And "The Men that are Falling" concludes:

The night wind blows upon the dreamer, bent
Over words that are life's voluble utterance.

You once recited Stevens to me, I am sure. Probably not that poem. And it was cold last night—no crickets. . . .

Now I've read the poem again. It's not really appropriate. Well, just a little appropriate. Oh, it doesn't matter!

You said you wanted me *to go further, next time.*

We had been kissing on a couch, in your parents' living room.

The carpet was beige, rather thick.

On the wall perpendicular to the couch: a piece of bread, framed, in gratitude: your father had been captured by the Germans, had barely survived.

The next evening we parked behind the Methodist Church. A dog barked once, twice, then settled down. Beyond the parking lot: a playground, then a high hedge. It was a secret spot, nearly perfect. Often we went there. I never told anyone, not even Dave, who, with Debbie, would park along the road overlooking the airport runway. *Going out to see the blue lights,* they called it. The Boeing 727s, it now occurs to me, must have come in— or flown out—right over them.

Now you are married and have a child. Perhaps you have several children. At least, you were married (and pregnant) the last time I saw you—at that coffee shop where my mother and I stopped one evening, for a piece of pie.

You tried to conceal your surprise by feigning surprise. As for me, our encounter, however tense, seemed at the same time expected, in the natural course of that day's events. Introductions were made; your husband, who seemed friendly, was wearing an orange golf shirt. I asked how your father was getting along—a squat, amiable man who a year or two before, although in his early fifties, had suffered a massive heart attack. *As if,* my mother had said to me at the time, *the captivity in Germany hadn't been enough for one man to bear.*

Finally, after saying *well, bye-bye,* you led your husband to a rather distant table.

My mother searched for her cigarettes and lighter. Almost immediately—as if she had surmised something— a waitress appeared, poured us each a cup of coffee. I could discern, through the weak, brownish liquid, the geometric design running along the inside rim of the cup. The design was, in its circularity, endless.

When they told you you couldn't have children, you drove back to your farm, parked your pick-up, fed your chickens, and had a beer. You were all alone in your house, as almost always, and the only noises came from the cooing, scratching, of the two turtle doves in their cage— but they soon quieted down—, and from your old she-cat, who nudged, nearly tipped over, a bowl of milk on the tile floor of the kitchen. You thought of putting on a record, a Santana album, but ended up simply sitting there, at your living-room table, a little longer.

You had exam papers to correct; tears rolled down your cheeks. You recalled one after another the various men you had loved, how you had broken off with some of them and how, more often, you had been forgotten, discarded. Once-cherished faces came to mind: the most recent, practically a boy, met on a trip to a faraway land; another, in longing for whom you had drunk an entire bottle of wine after you had received that improbable, hoped-for letter. Somehow, the coolness, darkness, stillness of that remote night was almost like this one. And there was a third, some time ago, a moustached man who, after some quick, boggled lovemaking, had slept in till noon. And a fourth, a husky, gregarious artist with a beard. And others.

Those loves had ended. No others seemed foreseeable. You were thirty-eight years old and, oh, if I had imagined all this—it would not have been difficult to do so—I would have broken my college-boy silence. Believe me. But our lives continued in parallel.

That time you invited me to your farm, you took off your shoes, walked barefoot across the lawn to feed your animals. It had not yet snowed, but it was the beginning of February. You shouted back over your shoulder: *I hate shoes!* Watching, I shivered in my too-light jacket. Inside your house, later, while we talked in the living room, it was not very warm either.

I think I will always try to remember you this way, your feet bare on the cold grass, on the cold soil, your hands tossing fodder to your chickens.

The dusk had blurred the hard edges.

Silence had fallen everywhere, in the surrounding fields, in the neighboring houses.

The sky was as heavy, as impenetrable, as the earth.

You moved through this dark, dormant world, your gestures quick, exact. The very existence of someone else, I thought—*your existence,* I murmured to myself, watching you sweep up some spilt grain—is a miracle.

You shouted something at one of your chickens.

Then you returned, and I asked if the calves had run there, just beyond the fence, as you had once written in a letter.

Yes.

You bit your lower lip.

You walked past me, to put away your pail.

Then we went inside, spoke at length about what had separated us. Later, we drove back to town, had dinner in a Chinese restaurant.

The Cantonese rice?—too dry. The little coconut cakes?—neglected. Like that other time when we had eaten in a Chinese restaurant, you ordered a second bottle of Tsing-Tao beer.

It's midnight, you eventually said.

We stepped outside into the icy, misty air. We said nothing more as I walked you to your car. Then I kissed your cheek. You got in, buckled your seat belt, waved, pulled away from the curb—too quickly.

I went down to the storage room this morning, looking for that box of old photographs.

And I found the box, after moving into the corridor a gas stove, a lounge chair, cartons of books, gardening equipment, paint cans, boards, various odds and ends.

Back in the apartment, I opened the box, but didn't find the photo I was looking for. I must have thrown it away long ago, probably that morning when I decided to leave the States for good.

*

Our picture had been taken in front of the entryway to a dance.

You were wearing a dress that perhaps your mother had made: orange pastel, or rose; rather shapeless; we were holding hands, both of us looking straight into the lens of the camera.

Nearly everything else I have forgotten.

Your last name eludes me.

Your father was an artist; he had abandoned you at an early age.

You were shy, and that quality was your charm.

Strangely, very early this morning—around four or five—I awoke with that photo in my mind.

I could see your face—close up.

For an instant, your features came to life, and I was moved.

I remembered your blue eyes, I remembered your eyebrows. I remembered the bridge of your nose.

I remembered your face coming up to mine (*I'm a little afraid,* you whispered), just as I was turning to kiss you, sitting in the front seat of Mike's car, snow by then having fully covered the windshield.

Like a teenager (I was twenty-two), I had written your name on my ink blotter.

Then, a few evenings later, after Geoff or Mike had given you the key, you slipped into our apartment. You left a plate of cookies on my desk. Your name on the ink blotter?—you must have seen it. Several of us were playing basketball at the gym. When I arrived home, I found the cookies. It seemed to be the confirmation. I rushed over to your house. You blushed, coming down the stairs.

Our love flared, burnt out just as quickly. Yes, in that final, chance encounter, what you said—that is, didn't say—was like a plate, not of chocolate-chip cookies, but of ashes.

These moments from twenty . . . no, exactly twenty-one years and four months ago. I have just come across your photo in an alumni magazine. If the photo is recent, you have hardly changed at all. (Yet there must be wrinkles at the corners of those light-green eyes.) Your married name belongs to no college acquaintance and, above all . . . this spelling of your first name. I must have known at the time, but, whenever I have thought of you over the years, I have always misspelled it: there is no final "e."

Strangely, now that I have corrected the spelling in my mind, you have lost your aura. I can imagine you walking down a street in San Francisco. I can imagine you raising children—but do you have any? I can imagine you playing Edgar Varèse on the flute (which I hope you haven't given up: the note in the alumni magazine mentioned your promotion to a position in marketing). You've become yourself once again—whoever you were and are.

I wanted our hands to touch, above the table.

We were sitting in a pastry shop, somewhere in Hamburg.

You had ordered a hot chocolate; so had I; it was ten o'clock in the morning; only two or three customers were about; the owner was reading *Die Welt,* which he had opened out over a counter.

Sunlight streamed in behind you, as the sun came out over the rooftops.

Or was that bright pool of light already there when we sat down?

I saw you in a halo of light.

And you placed your hand halfway across the table, your fingers somehow longer, thinner, than I had expected. A hand still adolescent after twenty years of living, the index finger scratching at the thumb's cuticle. From nervousness?

Had you read my thoughts? Why did you keep turning your eyes away?

Every time you turned your eyes away, I glanced at your hand, desiring to touch it.

As gently as possible.

And the dream ended.

I didn't know whether I could touch you, kiss you, caress you. Your roommate had gone to Freiburg for a few days. We had come up the two flights of stairs for tea. There was Saturday-night traffic in the avenue below. Through the gauze curtains, light from the streetlamps: long shadows on the ceiling. You turned on your desk lamp, then the neon over the sink.

Still talking enthusiastically about the film, you heated the water, searched for two cups, the honey jar, the tea bags. You kept your back turned to me most of the time. You were watching the tiny bubbles forming. I heard the water beginning to boil—a metallic sound. I imagined what it would be like to take hold of your shoulders, to turn you around, to kiss you, to caress your breasts. But I waited; that is, hesitated.

Someone wearing clogs pounded up the stairs. (Your roommate, returning home unexpectedly?) Tires screeched outside. Then silence set in once again before you turned and said: *Tea's ready.*

Pain was visible in her eyes, said my friend, *as she turned away from you.* I remembered your turning; I had not noticed your eyes.

We had shaken hands. I had stepped back, watched you search for your keys, find them, turn the key in the lock.

It was eight o'clock in the evening. François and I returned to his tiny Renault, which he had parked illegally in the Grindelallee.

We sat there waiting. The lights came on in your room on the second floor. We drove back to Othmarschen.

I had not noticed your eyes.

Later the scene came back to me. Again. And again. I remembered how you had turned. I remembered the thick blue wool of your coat—the sheen, reflected on it from a streetlight, as you turned. Slowly, but surely, I could see the pain in your eyes.

I lay in bed that Sunday morning, counting the bells tolling across the Binnenalster. It was eight o'clock in the morning. I covered my eyes with my forearm and imagined what I would tell you if we ever met again: that I had desired to caress your arms, kiss you tenderly: your eyelids, your hands. Would there be another meeting? The next day I was leaving.

I imagined us sitting on my single bed, our backs leaning against the wall. It was the end of the afternoon. The sunlight had left the window. With the white veil of curtains drawn, we were immersed in a sad, deep penumbra. Between us our fingers touched. I stroked your fingertips from time to time: the skin, the nails.

Often silence settled between my words and yours. A silence resembling my trembling caresses. Not a silence I wished to flee: a mysterious silence that united us. But the next day I was leaving.

You turned your head, looked into my eyes. The softness in your eyes. Neither of us knew how to continue. The next day, I was leaving.

I imagined myself knocking on your door. The door was painted a light shade of green. It was a student's room, on the fourth or fifth floor—I couldn't remember. You opened the door, we stood there looking at each other—for how long? A second? A minute? I marveled at how much affection had built up between us—in your eyes, in my eyes. . . .

Finally I said: *I thought of you so much I started wondering whether you really existed.*

Without saying a word, you reached out, took my hand, and drew me into the room.

*

I again imagined you in Paris, far away. Your hand was reaching to turn off the hot water. You dried your hands on a yellow—or orange—towel, to the right of the wash basin. Then you turned and walked back to your desk.

The afternoon silence in your small studio apartment. You were reading a book and taking notes. A book, as your letter had indicated, about Georg Büchner. I looked down at my postcard, which would be slid under your door.

Or into a letterbox with your name on it?

I imagined myself standing in the entryway of an apartment building. I was looking over the letterboxes for your name.

Upstairs, on the fourth—or fifth—floor, when I came in, your back was turned to me. You were reading.

Perhaps you would be away when the card arrived. On the métro? At a film? We had not said good-bye; we had somehow missed each other. Nothing had begun, nothing had ended.

I left my rented house in the Greek village. A steep path descended to the tiny square. Cobblestones, with donkey droppings here and there. A friendly old woman, on her doorstep, asked: *Pou pas? Where are you going?*

I pointed further down. That day, I walked all the way down to the sea.

*

I dreamt, awoke, then sought again to dream. Your face appeared, as did others. You were living far away. When I called you on the phone, you beckoned me to come at once; but when, after a long journey, I arrived and you came down a half-flight of stairs from a sort of mezzanine (where you had been sleeping on a mattress), you were someone else whom I also knew. I could no longer speak to this person in the same way that I was accustomed to speaking to you. Yet I tried. The person became you. This second dream, however, faded just as quickly. What did we say to each other *then?* I lost my ability to conjure you up. A silly thought, a wish, came to mind: you, too, were dreaming of me. And I wondered whether, somewhere in a space no longer accessible to us, we continued speaking to, or somehow gazing at, each other.

I imagined how we would meet at the Gare d'Austerlitz.
Our rendezvous was at the beginning of the quay.

As I approached, you finally saw me, began to smile.
I also began to smile. Immediately I felt the urge to hug
you, to kiss you on the lips. But when I stopped in front
of you I kissed you on both cheeks, as was our custom.

Yet our eyes looked, locked, into each other's. I set
down my two suitcases; when I straightened up we did
hug and ever so slowly our lips did meet. A short kiss at
first, followed by one tender one. It was the first time.

What is happening to us? I asked, but it seemed there
would be no answer for hours, weeks, months—ever?

The passengers hurried by, someone jostled us, we
laughed and were happy; the cold drafts of air, the noise,
the hustle and bustle of the station. We were happy!

And we had already started knowing what was hap-
pening to us.

I awoke at four in the morning, got out of bed, went to the bathroom, emptied my bladder of its warm urine. As I crawled back into bed, my body temperature dropped. I shivered once, twice. I pulled the covers up to my shoulders. My allergies flared. I sneezed. . . . Once again I arose (so as not to bother you with further sneezing), went to my study, found a handkerchief, looked over my books for Robert Walser's *Dreams*.

I blew my nose thoroughly.

In the living room, I read.

I tried to concentrate on every word.

Yet the lamp was dim, and I had left my glasses on the bedside table. I had moreover forgotten my German dictionary. I gazed into the near-darkness filling the rest of the room. Then I began thinking of Walser's life and the well-known photo of him hiking through the snow. Not really his body . . . rather something like a tangible abstraction of his former bodily existence—a configuration of matter, in motion, during a lifetime—passed before my eyes. The configuration—representing the man, the writer—twinkled like a constellation of heroic stars, before a sadness beyond telling—a cloud—passed over all the pinpoints of light.

I leafed through the book, reading passages here and there. He had written—had he really dreamt?—about hiking near a mountain town.

My thoughts drifted to vacations that we had spent in the Alps.

One morning, leaving Bessans, we had followed an unpaved forest-service road. It was leading up the Vallée du Riban. The night before, we had seen a slide show during which the commentator had mentioned a pair of eagles that were nesting in the same valley. Remembering the eagles as we progressed along the road, and eyeing the not-so-distant peaks, I wondered on which rocky crag they were nesting—perhaps tearing at that very moment into the flesh of some rodent or, as apparently could happen, into the tender muscles of a small lamb.

The road was rising; the valley was narrowing to a gorge.

It was—at least had been—sunny; the dark cliffs on each side oppressed us; soon we were enveloped in endless shadows.

We turned back. We passed, once again, the charming patch of Turk's-cap. We sought refuge in the village with its carved wooden balconies. We had lunch in the hotel bordering the square. Then we bought groceries for our evening meal, revisited the small museum at the church, and returned to read in our rented room at The Snow Hamlet.

When I glanced at you, you suddenly seemed eighty years old. The metamorphosis was difficult to accept, but, as you didn't look up from your book, I forced myself to contemplate you in your old age. Tiny hairs had sprouted under your chin. Wrinkles had spread from the corners of your eyes. And the line formed between your lips veered at each end downwards, bent by time almost into a frown.

You continued to read. I watched your eyes blinking. I felt sorry, saddened, that you had aged so quickly, unexpectedly . . . and just as soon I imagined myself leaning over, kissing you on the cheek—your chapped, unpowdered skin.

I held myself back. I kept examining your face, observing how beauty is lost, feeling increasingly in the presence of the mystery that linked your life to mine. What was this mystery? It did not involve your perishable beauty—this I had known all along.

Then you looked up, and I, too, had reached the last years of my life.

Seven Apperceptions

One Night's Wind

One night I thought again that I might die in not too long a time. The wind was beating against the wooden shutters—rolled down tightly over the windows. We tossed and turned, speaking from time to time. Morning came suddenly, with the alarm.

I have not forgotten a certain sensation—while I was pushing the button on the alarm clock that next morning, while I was remembering that the wind had beaten against the wooden shutters, as if against my life.

And some mornings, ever since, I listen for remembrances of that one night's wind, as I slowly crank the wooden shutters upwards, even onto mornings bathed in rosy light.

The Train Station

I was with three friends. We were in Europe. We were hurrying to catch a train.

One of the friends was Dick Wittenbroodt. Another was Charlie. I could not establish the identity of the third friend.

Upon arriving at the station, Dick and the other friend ran to the departures board to learn our platform number. Charlie, however, led me out of the station and into the freight yard, where he wanted to show me a new kind of boxcar. We went over to the boxcars—they were refrigerator boxcars—and examined them for quite some time. Our hands were in our pockets. We had turned our collars up to our ears. It was cold.

By the time we returned to the station, our friends— let alone the train we were supposed to take—had vanished. In fact, no trains stood at the platforms. No passengers were waiting. The entire station was deserted. The station, partly destroyed as if by bombs, seemed to have been abandoned several years previously, perhaps after a war.

The government has probably not yet allocated the funds necessary to reconstruct the station, I remarked to Charlie.

But when I turned to him, anticipating his response, he too had vanished.

I wandered out of the station, returned to the freight yard, walked between the refrigerator boxcars. I wondered if I could—should—become a hobo. But were there any trains left, to hop? Were there any train engineers? I walked on, eventually leaving the freight yard behind. The tracks I was following led into the country. Thistle-like weeds had sprouted high between the ties. Also a sort of milkweed—at least a plant I identified as such. To my left, to my right, lay ditches full of stagnant water. There was not the slightest tremor on their scumy surfaces. I gazed beyond the ditches, at untilled fields extending as far as my eyes could see.

And straight ahead? The tracks curved ever so little. The two rusty rails narrowed, at the horizon, into a point.

Hometown

Walking to an appointment, I got lost in my hometown. The landmarks had been bulldozed away. Keosauqua Way was a graded field. And, in the distance, the building at which my father had worked for forty years was a toppled ruin, exactly like the Temple of Zeus in Athens.

I sought out pedestrians—*hikers*—, but there were none. The workers seemed to be having a day off. Enormous machines lay about. At last I came across a telephone booth standing near the spot where, I estimated, had been located the stereo shop owned by the uncle of a girl with whom I had been in love decades before—in fifth grade?—, but when I lifted the receiver, put in some small change, a dial tone sounded briefly, followed by absolute silence.

The sky was cloudless, light-blue. Perhaps—probably—it was winter. Or early spring. Here and there in front of me shimmered puddles of water, frozen-over. The leveled earth was not the rich black soil I remembered, but rather a clayish, hard, light-brown surface. I set off once again on my subarctic expedition, noticing that even the toppled ruin had now disappeared.

Where was I heading? With whom exactly was I still trying to keep an appointment? With a doctor? With my father? With the little girl? I no longer knew for sure. An icy wind gusted up, seemingly out of nowhere.

I trod ever further across this wind-swept, barren landscape, keeping my head down, my gloveless hands in my pockets, my parka barely fending off the cold, although now and then I did discover cast-off artefacts—a belt buckle, a plastic trinket, a ball-point pen, a colored rubber band. I persevered, no other landmark, goal or even horizon in sight.

The Latin Lesson

When I entered the kitchen (which resembled the kitchen in our second family house), I found my father reading through a small stack of newspaper clippings. With him, crowded around the cherry-wood table, were my sister Joan, a few neighbors who were not from the second but rather from our first neighborhood, as well as other purported *acquaintances* and *friends* whom I did not know or, probably, could no longer recognize. (I had lived for nearly two decades in France.) As it turned out— so my father informed me with a mixture of seriousness and embarrassment—, the clippings were reviews of a new book I had written about Des Moines (but this time with a title in Latin). I asked my father if the reviews were good; his hesitating, affirmative reply implied that several nasty ones lurked in the bunch.

I quipped that the best thing that could happen to me would be a savage attack in one of the widely-leafed-through supplements. No one in the group, drinking daiquiris and reading the lukewarm—at best—reviews, added anything to that remark. The silence was cathedral. Over a shoulder—Ruth's; she had come back to life—, I perused a few paragraphs of a surprisingly generous article. The critic conceded that *a certain mystery prevails in the reader's mind. This is no mean accomplishment,* he added, *for all the characters are slight and there is no plot whatsoever.* I searched for the critic's name. His surname—the ink was smudged and I couldn't make out his first name—was my own. Reproduced alongside another review (held in the hands of a woman who, it now occurs to me, must have been Jeannie) was a photograph of my other sister, Ann. She had been interviewed as one of the main protagonists. . . . Yet before I could read what Ann had to say, I awoke. My hand automatically groped across the bedside table. Where was the book I had supposedly written? What Latin title had I given it? I thought of Mrs. Brinkman, my ninth-grade Latin teacher, wondering if she were still alive. I calculated her age. I reckoned with the actuarial probabilities. Then I arose to urinate. It was three in the morning. When I returned to bed, I lay as quietly as I could, troubled by the image of Mrs. Brinkman returning from the dead, approaching the bed, bending down and whispering—as she would, in the hallway, during passing periods—*salve.*

An Artist-Friend

An artist-friend had died and a few of us had gathered, months, perhaps even a year later, in his small country house overlooking a stream. His widow was not there. I wanted to ask Denis, standing nearby, how she was doing, but, strangely, I couldn't remember her name.

Then I remembered: it was Flavia. I recalled the boeuf bourguignon that Françoise and I had eaten with them, years and years before in Paris. My friend, who liked to cook (but only cooked rarely), had spent an entire day preparing it.

She's fine, I overheard someone saying, *still making candles and taking care of the children.*

What children? I wondered, not daring to ask, knowing only of two girls, from my friend's first marriage, who were now in their late twenties. *And what candles?* Flavia, at last word, was teaching Italian to businessmen.

Across the room someone else—who seemed to be a critic or perhaps a professor of art history—was speaking about an exhibition of our late friend's paintings. *Maybe we could organize one,* he suggested, making a broad gesture towards us. There was apparently going to be a colloquium, at the Sorbonne, devoted to reggae music—*and that would be an auspicious occasion,* he stated.

The critic's (or the professor's) pomposity, rather out of keeping with the ambience of our commemoration and thus enigmatic, made me ask myself: *Am I dreaming?* And at just that moment, Justin, in the adjoining room, cried out.

I turned on the light: it was 6:14 in the morning.

Whenever he cries out like that, I do not get up immediately. Sometimes it is a nightmare, sometimes he has momentarily lost his stuffed rabbit.

Justin cried out again and, when I came into his room, he was standing in his crib.

Two hours later, after having fed him his cereal and changed his diaper, after having built a block tower with him and read him his favorite books, after having washed his face with rosewater and cleaned his runny nose, after having dressed him in clothes that Françoise had freshly ironed, after having put on his socks and shoes, after having pushed him in his stroller to the day care center, I recalled another scene from my dream: we had all walked down a narrow path (with grass on each side) from the house to the stream. There was a full moon. The moonlight was glistening on the water. . . .

I pushed a button. The front door of our apartment building opened. Turning left, I entered the little room where the letter boxes stand.

A newspaper from the States, a bank statement.

I said good morning to the cleaning lady, who was mopping the entryway, then snuck (avoiding a talkative neighbor) around the corner to the elevator, hoping no one else would join me there, thinking I would give my artist-friend a call later in the day and, for the time being, anticipating that mysterious communion that would be mine when, all alone, riding up to the eighth floor, I would once again perceive the glistening moonlight on the stream.

Autumnal

Little matter what guides me to that window over-looking the gently flowing river. I am standing there, my fingertips on the sill, and below me stretches to the horizon my hometown in its autumnal colors. Houses emerge through the towering trees—oaks, maples. They have shed half their leaves. Not the slightest noise rises to me, so high in the air.

Yes, I must always try to remember that tiny hospital waiting room—a coffee machine against the wall, magazines strewn about on a low table, issues long out-of-date, the covers torn away from the binding staples or torn off completely. I sat there for hours every day, during one entire week, holding a novel in my hand.

In the waiting room, at the window, my fingertips on the sill, I look down on the gently flowing river. My hometown stretches to the horizon in its autumnal colors. Or perhaps it is not my hometown. I turn my ear in the direction of the river and imagine the sound of the water delicately lapping against the muddy banks.

*

Sometimes I wonder what my mother thinks, would think, of Justin. But she died in 1981. And Justin was born eleven years later, in France. He plays in the sand at the day-care center and, when I open the gate, he crawls towards me.

There is an evergreen tree—a pine? a cedar?—near my mother's grave in Des Moines.

Justin raises his right hand, puts it down, raises his left hand—he is parodying the act of crawling. He stops, squats back on his heels, looks up at me, and bursts out laughing.

He points to things, one after the other. He already knows his way home, indicating turns. When flocks of pigeons fly overhead, he follows them with his eyes—until they disappear.

Near the cedar tree, or the pine tree, near my mother's grave, a few oak and maple leaves have surely fallen as well. Yesterday, in the avenue Jeanne-d'Arc, we let Justin crawl through the plane-tree leaves. They were yellow, still wet from the storm.

Besse

We have explored the sleeping mountain town, touching walls hewn from basalt, dipping our fingers into the chilly fountain, and on our way back across the dimly-lit parking lot—on the edge of the medieval *cité*—I look up and immediately see how clear the night sky is. Sparkling above us: the Big Dipper, the Little Dipper, Orion, the Charioteer . . . the Pleiades. I get down on my knees so as to show Justin better. I put my cheek next to his, point up at the hazy cluster perched like a beacon near Perseus. *What does "beacon" mean?* he asks. And all I can answer is that—ever since I was a little boy—I have thought of the Pleiades as a sort of flashlight, in the sky. Or rather: as a lot of flashlights bundled together. And Justin adds that now that he is a big boy, he wakes up and reaches for his frog flashlight, pushes the button, and finds his way all by himself out of his dark bedroom.

Into the Waves

Tout ce qu'il fallait décrire hier
pour exister encore
et tout ce qu'il fallait rejoindre pour aimer.

("Everything that had to be described yesterday
so I could continue to exist
and everything that had to be rejoined so I could love.")

—Jean-Philippe Salabreuil

As a child I had heard my mother talk so often about Seaside that it was as if I myself had stayed there summer after summer, for vacation. I could imagine the board-walk, the beach at high or low tide, the sand and salt in the wind, the sunsets in July, digging for clams, but more than these Seaside was the taste—the texture—of salt-water taffy, *chewy, chewy, chewy, chewy.* Every August, at the Iowa State Fair, my mother would buy a box of what she considered *not really the same thing but close enough so you'll know what I'm talking about,* and whenever she took out a piece she would reminisce about the weeks she had spent on the beach as a youngster, then as a teenager, before the Second World War and just afterwards. The saltwater taffy was sold in a special shop along the boardwalk—or in a back street?—and dur-ing the fall my mother and my grandmother would make the taffy at home, pulling and stretching the strands on the back porch. *Pulling the taffy is extremely important,* my mother insisted. I never understood why we couldn't make saltwater taffy in Des Moines—pulling and stretching it on our back porch—, let alone go to Seaside for the summer.

We finally did go to Seaside, but by then it was far too late for me to see the Pacific with those wide-open, as-tonished eyes that in the best of worlds every child would have upon coming across a natural wonder—however great or modest—for the first time. I was much more impressed, one afternoon in Greenwood Park, when suddenly I spotted a walkingstick in a bush. And much more impressed by other unexpected marvels: a hum-mingbird hovering over a blossom in our backyard; the yellowish color of the sky, one afternoon when the tor-nado siren blew; the ice and icicles everywhere, during the Great Ice Storm; or the Mississippi at Davenport, when my father and I crossed a seemingly endless bridge while driving to Chicago for a long weekend all by ourselves.

Seaside I had already imagined for years—regular rows of sparkling, white-crested waves rolling into the shore; a noisy, crowded beach strewn with parasols, volleyball nets and sand castles; a delicate maritime breeze, spring-like in the midst of summer—, and indeed I had imagined this scene so intensely that when I looked out on the same beach, for the first time, one July morning when I was about to turn fourteen, I felt a little disappointed. Was this because the real beach corresponded exactly—or not quite—to what I had anticipated? Or because the morning was overcast, the beach deserted and melancholic? All I remember is the initial disappointment. It was just a glimpse, anyway; we got back into the car, drove on, looking for our cottage.

I was quite a swimmer back then, so this initial disappointment actually mattered little. Most of all, I was eager to verify what it was like to swim in the ocean. Verify, because swimming in the ocean I had also long imagined. I had learned how to swim in pools: a private pool behind the house of a friend of my mother's, on the south side of town; then the steamy YMCA pool, downtown; the vast outdoor pool in Northwest Park, completed the year I entered junior high; and that tiny outdoor pool at the Country Club in Lewiston—a day's drive from Seaside—, where my maternal grandparents lived and where we spent our summer vacations. I had never swum in a lake or river, as my friends had; my mother would not allow it. Gray's Lake. Okoboji. The Raccoon. Not to mention swimming at the Pits—but my secret urge to observe what went on there arose much later, when I was in high school—, an ill-frequented, artificial pond formed by backwater channeled into an abandoned quarry, known for its midnight orgies, loose girls and occasional daylight drownings.

So for years I had imagined swimming in the ocean. And in the ocean meant at Seaside. When I was quite young, say seven or nine, I would do my imagining—my experimenting—in the bathtub. I would fill up the tub as far as I dared, stretching out until my head rested on the back end and the water came up to my chin. Then, from this position, I would watch how my penis remained floating, upright, the glans just visible. With my right hand I would make waves, observing how the glans buoyed about. I had the impression that in the ocean I would buoy about similarly. Sometimes, while making waves, I would hold my penis in my left hand, noticing how it resisted. Seemingly detachable while remaining attached, my penis has never seemed entirely a part of my body.

This propensity to imagine what life presumably promises characterized my earliest years, my adolescent years, my young adult years, and still characterizes me, alas. Sometimes I think that to date I have only rarely experienced the present, having instead spent my life perpetually envisioning what conceivably could happen, or else what might have happened had this or that word been pronounced, this or that gesture been made. How many times I have rewritten history, bringing it up to an utterly different present, knowing how the slightest change in a detail, the slightest shift in perspective, can change everything. Not to mention my constant acting-out of the future, rehearsing my self-assigned role over and over until I am confident that I will be able to overcome, when the big day comes, stage fright.

When I was four, a serious illness had kept me shut up in a hospital, then in our house, for months, and perhaps my inability, at any given moment, to disengage myself from the future or from the past dates from the dull green walls of that polio ward in Methodist Hospital or from my room upstairs—stuffy, oblong, with its one window at the end. The outside world had disappeared, been re-established at an imaginable, yet otherwise unattainable remove. During my convalescence, I would listen: my childhood playmates were running about, beneath the window. Nancy was shouting something. Steve was shouting back. Maybe that was Goodwin crying. And I would imagine their games, imagine myself playing. Later, when I had recovered, it was too late. Like the others I would play tag, blindman's buff, hide-and-go-seek, but while playing I could not keep myself from remembering how, months before, I had already imagined myself running, chasing, hiding, reaching out to touch—in exactly the same way. Or not quite. No, it was not quite the same, now that I was really playing. As when, later, I finally saw Seaside, I was a little let down. I would continue going through the motions—running, chasing, hiding, reaching out to touch—, but my attention was now riveted on that slight disappointment, on those subtle differences between the ongoing present and my once-imagined future now also a present going on. Running, chasing, hiding, reaching out to touch—but I was ever searching for my former, profounder emotion.

It must have been during my convalescence that my mother first talked to me about Seaside. Of this I am almost sure. *And what you'll like most of all is running into the waves until you fall down,* she would say, rubbing my weary, feverish legs with alcohol—the coolness of that alcohol, the firmness of her hands moving over my thighs and calves. The idea of battling the waves both panicked and exalted me. I tried to feel the force, the heaviness, of the tons of water. My shins against the tons of water. I dashed into the sea. Eventually—soon?—I fell, vanquished. *Some day I'll take you there,* my mother was adding, explaining how the road passed around the Blue Mountains, ran along the Columbia, through Portland, then on to the coast. I had the impression that a trip to Seaside was going to be my reward, if I recovered.

My mother's childhood trips to Seaside took one hot, interminable day of driving. It was my grandmother who drove, never my grandfather, for in fact he always stayed behind in Lewiston, working, a habit my uncles adopted once he had gotten Parkinson's disease and they had taken over his real-estate business. *The men in the family* (as my mother and grandmother would say) never took vacations, and even my father (I suspect) only reluctantly left his work behind in Des Moines to take us out west every summer. When Ann, Joan and I were very young, my mother would take us out to Idaho on the train—the Great Northern or the Northern Pacific—, and how I remember with emotion those magnificent panoramic dome cars; the stern but ever helpful bell-ringing stewards; the bunk beds in our private compartments; the silverware and white tablecloths in the dining cars; the scary passageways between cars with those constantly moving steel panels at our feet; not to forget that mysterious clickety-clack of the wheels in the middle of the night when, so sleepy, I would fight against myself to stay awake. Years later, I would fight against myself in many other ways. We would stay in Lewiston for most of the summer, my father joining us for a couple of weeks in early August.

How did my mother spend her days at Seaside? She spoke about swimming in the sea, about laying out on the sand and reading books, about playing volleyball; also about riding tandems up and down the boardwalk, with her younger brother Bob. As my mother reminisced, I would imagine them renting the tandems at the cluttered bicycle shop located next door to the place where the taffy was made. But was there a bicycle shop next door to the taffy-maker's? Whenever I asked my mother to explain, she would answer: *Oh, I don't really remember. Somewhere along the boardwalk.* Or was the shop I imagined simply a replica of the one on 24th Street, in Des Moines, where I had picked out my first bike, a green Schwinn? It was on my eighth birthday that my father took me there—a long, narrow shop exuberantly crowded with bicycles old and new, dozens hanging down from the ceiling. The owner, an old man with grease on his hands, tousled my hair, then negotiated with my father. Once in a while, afterwards, we returned; for a small adjustment in the chain, for a new reflector, for streamers. Then that shop disappeared. And the entire building was razed.

As a child I felt a need, which was not always assuaged, to localize precisely my mother's anecdotes, to envision the street layout of Seaside in its most minute details, to be able to trace out in my mind her every itinerary, from the cottage to the beach, from the beach to the sea, from the sea back to her towel, from her rolling up of the towel and her placing it under her arm to her strolling with my grandmother through the back streets as they shopped for dinner or, perhaps, for nothing in particular at all. I would imagine my mother lingering at a brightly arrayed window. I would imagine my mother and my grandmother entering a shop and buying a light, cottony dress. *Blue. Your father will be so happy,* my grandmother would exclaim. Then she would call out through the crowds at my uncle Bob—my uncle

John, my mother's older brother, rarely participated in these scenes—to *come right back over here!* They would walk on a little farther. *Oh, he's wandered off again!* my grandmother would sigh, then shake her head theatrically as if secretly satisfied—with him? With herself? Such scenes had taken place—so I knew, but this knowledge troubled me—well before I was born.

Because of my mother's stories, I was intrigued by the question of what riding a tandem was like. My parents had never rented one for us, neither in Lewiston nor in Des Moines. But did I ever plead with them to rent one? Probably I kept my desire bottled up inside, like so often, later. Perhaps I mentioned it once, twice, and the subject was changed. Little matter; graver activities intrigued me more. Yet one autumn day, Marilyn and Debbie had two tandems waiting when Tom and I showed up for our secret rendezvous—one of those graver activities—at Witmer Park. They had wanted to surprise us; surprise me they did and, picturing my mother riding a tandem at Seaside, I suddenly felt very nervous. Tom, as debonair as usual, took the unexpected twist in stride. (*Make sure you're the one who calls the shots,* he had often advised me.) Full of confidence, he slung his arm around Marilyn, kissed her on the lips. Marilyn closed her eyes; the kiss lasted for quite some time. . . . Tom kept adjusting the angle of his aim, ardently. I observed him, as one observes a true master. Was I supposed to kiss Debbie? We barely knew each other. Yet of course I had imagined kissing her, an act that both fascinated and terrified me: I had never kissed a girl before. I stood there, watching her out of the corner of my eye, worrying. Eventually she told me to get on the tandem, up front. Relieved, disappointed, I obeyed. Then she got on and we pushed off—

wobbingly, precariously. We gathered momentum with great difficulty. She screamed something I didn't understand. I was concentrating on pedaling with all my force. Debbie kept shouting orders. I felt encumbered, overburdened with that gigantic contraption, wondering how my mother had managed to have so much fun. Wouldn't it have been better to walk through the park, holding hands?

In a while I did get the tandem under control. I even took one hand from the handlebars and started pointing out trees to Debbie. *No, over there, not the honey locust, the burr oak. That one—do you see the reddish one?—is a Schwedler's maple. . . .* It was the year of my great leaf collection for science class. *Let's stop and wait for Tom and Marilyn,* I suggested, realizing Debbie was getting bored with dendrology.

Was I, too, getting bored—with Debbie? Or somehow exasperated? A little weary? Was I only tired of the tandem? Or was I now in fact even more fascinated than before, realizing at last what all along had been evident: that we were not, as she said, *the same?* We rode on silently for a while; I felt Debbie's presence behind me, so close to me, as if it were a vast mystery. I was attracted to the mystery, so attracted I soon wished to envelop myself in it once again, but not so deeply this time. I desired to dip in, then slip back slightly, so as to contemplate it from a safer remove. I wanted to both touch and contemplate the mystery. Why Debbie? Why not Marilyn? Or any other girl, for that matter? I wanted to love—to be in love with—Debbie, but did wanting to love mean loving? Can love come into being otherwise than spontaneously? And if my love for Debbie had indeed unexpectedly welled up, a few weeks before in algebra class, why these questions now? Here we were together, at last all alone. *I want to love you, Debbie.* I chased away the implications of what I had come to understand—about myself. We successfully brought the heavy tandem to a halt. We looked over our shoulders. Tom and Marilyn were nowhere in sight. All afternoon we rode around Witmer, searching for our friends on those densely-shaded, winding streets: Maquoketa, Germania, Lakewood, Forestdale. Eventually I had to leave; Debbie agreed to wait, with the tandem, on Marilyn's front steps. It was time to get home. My mother, thinking I was playing touch football, was expecting me at five.

Our trip to Seaside took place, not that coming summer, but the summer after that. Now almost fourteen, I strangely felt younger as we arrived in town: nine, ten, no older than eleven or twelve. And thinking about Seaside today, I again feel much younger (four, nine, ten, fourteen . . .) but also for the first time old, *forty being the traditional milestone,* as my father put it recently on a birthday card. Yes, from four to forty, thoughts of Seaside: perplexing, disquieting thoughts. And often I have written in an attempt to unpuzzle them; or to answer other, troubling, persistent questions; or to overcome at last certain obstacles; and always to grasp again, for less ephemeral instants, a fragment of what so quickly I have traversed. Sometimes I imagine my past life—my memory of it—as a vast oblivion resembling the sea, spotted with mysterious islands, with inexplicable reefs, with impregnable boulders broken off from the craggy coast. The sea at Seaside: as much the outside world I was dreaming of during my childhood, as my inner world—then and now.

For once, we didn't have to search for a hotel. My father's colleague had supposedly helped us rent *a nice little cottage with a view,* such as my grandmother would rent for those vacations with my mother and her two brothers *way back when*. The address my mother was holding in her lap, however, turned out to be that of a motel—pink-painted, concrete, cubic, three or four stories high. A narrow neon sign, featuring the name of the motel and a small pink bear, ran down the entire length of the building. In addition the motel—the Pink Bear Motel—was set back two streets from the seafront and at the far, southern end of the beach, quite a way from the boardwalk. *It's not at all like it used to be here*, remarked my mother for the first time that day.

The motel manager handed my father the key; we soon entered a spacious apartment: a living room, three bedrooms, a kitchen. We all agreed, even my mother: *This is not bad at all*. Ann let herself fall back on the couch, testing the springs. She nearly bounced back to her feet, and burst out giggling. She fell back again, bounced back up. My mother calmed us down, gave orders. I lugged the ice cooler in all by myself and set it down in the bathtub, to drain.

While on vacation, my mother worried constantly about ice—whether the ice in the cooler had already melted, whether we would be able to fill the cooler back up once we had found a place to sleep for the night. And what did we keep in the cooler? Milk for breakfast, cheese and baloney for our sandwiches the next day, sometimes a yogurt or two, my mother foregoing her beloved tuna-fish sandwiches with mayonnaise (not to mention her other favorite: grilled-cheese sandwiches) for the entire duration of our scorching hot drives across the Great Plains and Rocky Mountains. We shopped in the evening, in a supermarket, for the next day's meal. My mother always made sure that everything was *ready for tomorrow*. She also anticipated the future and dwelled on the past, even more elaborately than I did.

Coincidentally (and fortunately for my mother), it was during those years that ice machines began appearing not only in gas stations, but also in motels all across the United States. If there was no ice machine in the motel alongside which we had just pulled up and hurriedly got out—the vacancy sign still posted outside; seven, eight o'clock at night—, my father would look at me tensely, wearily, then turn back to the man behind the desk: *Just a moment, sir, I need to talk to the rest of the family.* Both of us knew, despite whatever other comforts we had noticed (a washing machine; a hot-drinks machine; a swimming pool, although Ann, Joan and I were never allowed to swim in one), that the chances of staying in that particular motel were slim. Back down the highway we would roll, sometimes for over an hour. At my mother's window, my father: *It looks clean. The man says there's a good diner next door.* My mother: *Is there an ice machine for the cooler?* My mother did become more flexible—putting off shopping for the next day until the next day—when, after one such negotiation, we were only able to find a room in another motel three hours later, at midnight. That was our notorious stopover in Shelby: rats in the gutters; drunken, raucous ranchers in the trucker's café where we grabbed a greasy bite to eat; my father and I sleeping on the filthy carpet: there was only one double bed in the room. That was not the summer we went to Seaside.

At the Pink Bear Motel there were five neatly-made beds in our suite and, downstairs near the office, an ice machine. The ice machine was even outfitted with two chutes—two buckets could be filled simultaneously—and with a series of buttons regulating the size of the crushed ice. Ann started trying out all the options, from cubes to slush, but fairly quickly—as if in anticipation of pranksters like herself—the machine flashed an unambiguous message: *No more ice available.* We read a note scotch-taped onto the machine: *If no more ice is available, come back in an hour. But you have to wait at least two hours,* complained Ann. She was speaking from experience. *Otherwise, the cubes are frozen on the outside and full of water inside.*

Back in the apartment, as Ann, Joan and I were unpacking our things, we heard a cry: my mother had found silverfish in the bathroom. We all rushed over to look. Sure enough, one or two stragglers of the patrol were still slinking underneath the edge of the carpet, where it ran up against the bathtub. I stomped my foot along the edge of the carpet. *That'll kill most of them,* I exclaimed, but my mother was already elsewhere, thirty years before, at a Seaside without silverfish slithering underneath carpets. And yet there must have been silverfish back then, as well as—my mother did not stay long in her dreamworld—*this dampness, here, touch this wall.* She beckoned my father over. In a moment, we found silverfish in the kitchen.

Strangely, we got over the silverfish crisis rather soon. My father encouraged my mother to be philosophical. *Jan,* he said, *it's humid near the ocean. We're bound to have silverfish.* My mother contended they had never been infested with insects back then, *in the cottage,* but, true to her nature, she did not carry the argument much further, withdrawing into herself and pouting outwardly. That the silverfish were our fault, her pouting made clear; especially our father's fault. After a tense moment of indecision, we all found something to do. I opened a drawer, reached into my suitcase for a T-shirt, then hesitated when a thought occurred to me: maybe silverfish also lurked in the cracks where the panels of wood had been fitted together. My father finally broke the silence by suggesting that he and I drive back into town and buy a can of insecticide.

But when are we going swimming? I asked.

This question roused my mother out of her sullenness. Suddenly in full charge of this part of our vacation (for otherwise it was my father and I who planned the trips, choosing the itineraries and all the sights we intended to visit), she embarked upon a long explanation of tides—the same explanation I had heard for years—, the dangers of swimming at low tide, the undertows, the quicksand, the possibility of an unexpected *falling-off* (by which she meant those places where the gradual slope of the beach broke off into a cliff), not to forget her conviction that certain aggressive sea creatures dwelling too far out to be reached at high tide could nonetheless be encountered at low tide, especially by an accomplished swimmer tempted to venture ever outwards, *well beyond his depth*. What exactly these aggressive sea creatures were, however, was never made explicit. My mother seemed to be talking about sharks. Yet soon she was exaggerating the real probabilities of meeting up with sharks at Seaside and giving legendary dimensions to the perils awaiting us. Listening to her, I imagined myself buoying about in the sea, a good two hundred yards from the shore, but despite her descriptions it was not mythical sea monsters or enormous sharks that were attacking me; rather, small, viciously carnivorous fish; minuscule octopuses wrapping their sucking tentacles around my fingers and toes; crustaceans piercing my abdomen with their bony spines; tiny jellyfish mortally stinging me. What I feared was not gigantic, but small, even at times microscopic, and was noticeable, foreseeable, only after the greatest efforts of concentration. The opaqueness of the sandy-salty, blue-gray sea. How could I swim and simultaneously remain vigilant? Decidedly, I would not swim out very far, not even at high tide.

At the same time, while my mother was talking, I sought to identify myself with those boys who inevitably would venture *well beyond their depths*—out of rashness, out of bravery, and with, in their muscular bodies, a stamina and strength surpassing my own. No, identify is not the right word. Did I admire them? Envy them? These words do not seem right, either. Having brought these boys into existence, in my mind, I envisioned myself treading water at a safe distance, neither too close to nor too far from the shore, while watching their every move. Their world was one of action; the entire world seemed one of action; my world, one of action imagined, at best observed. Action more often imagined than observed. Imagined and vaguely yearned for. Sometimes painfully yearned for. Sometimes desperately yearned for. I could not know then, while my mother was preparing us for our first swim in the sea, that ten years later, having settled in Samos, I would one day watch Greek boys racing each other back to the beach, pulling and pushing and splashing each other out of the water, boisterously comparing their jellyfish stings. Their shoulders, arms and legs—tattooed with bright red welts.

A few nights after watching those boys I resolutely joined a group of German students who had decided to go swimming in the Aegean, at midnight. We had been drinking ouzos together, in a large coffeehouse facing the harbor. We paid up, headed out; the beach was a couple of miles from town. From the top of the hill I saw a streetlamp still illuminating the sheltered crescent of sand. Arriving at the deserted beach, the Germans hurriedly took off all their clothes, ran laughing into the water, plunged in, swam out. I had watched the breasts of the girls, the penises of the boys, joyously flopping up and down. Then I too took off my clothes, strode into the cold water. I did not walk, I tried to stride. Was there a full moon? A night sky full of stars? My utter nudity; the cold sea water enveloping my genitals; my Seaside fears of jellyfish, lobsters, octopuses, piranahs. I tried to relax. I knew what I was afraid of, and why. I tried to relax. I swam the breast stroke, calmly, my hands and forearms pushing, pulling through the water, my head above the water, my eyes fixed on my companions straight ahead. They too were swimming the breast stroke. No one was speaking anymore; the world had taken on a close, dense stillness. Our naked bodies advanced gently through the close, dense stillness. Close. Dense. Stillness. A full moon? A starry night? Every now and then I discovered I had relaxed, for a few seconds. Then I would remember Seaside, my fears. Quite a way out into the shimmering, silent, waveless bay we swam.

My parents took us to the beach after lunch, once the tide had come in and we had almost finished digesting our meal. My mother was very strict about the *one-hour rule: A meal needs to be digested for at least an hour before you can go swimming.* She repeated this rule aloud, verified that it had been respected, every single time we went swimming in Des Moines, in Lewiston, anywhere. *Otherwise, you can get a stomach cramp,* she would warn us, *and maybe drown.* Convulsions, my body wrenching into a paralyzed V, sinking, sinking, sinking to the bottom.

A sandy bottom, seaweeds everywhere, the vestiges of a shipwreck. *Now I lay me down to sleep.* I murmured this prayer to myself, arranging my body as comfortably as possible amidst the weeds and the rusty wreckage.

From my earliest years I have often secretly envisioned my death—usually a violent end, sometimes by my own hand, but at the same time always observed from a certain distance, from outside myself, and with a curiosity surprisingly serene. During these moments death frightens me less than it intrigues. I am no longer but an infinitesimal particle of the universe; no longer a soul presumed independent of matter; but rather an entity composed only of matter, a strictly material entity having taken on an individual human configuration only momentarily. And this is a comforting thought, relieving me of a vast burden. Yes, living was a burden, I think, then imagine in slow motion the mortal shot, blow, leap leaving me crumbled on the pavement. Sometimes anonymous spectators gather round; little is said; there is no horror at all. Everything happens naturally. In my mind I rehearse these otherwise gruesome scenes, not going so far however as to put an end—neither in the observer's nor in the victim's mind—to my, his, their, our curiosity about them: to put an end to it all. To the very end, and thereafter, I remain curious. Which means that it is not I who have died. Which means that, in my mind, there is no real end. No, no end. Oh, I have always known all too well that while imagining my death I am not really, entirely, engaged with it.

Say that the beach at Seaside that afternoon was not very crowded. Say that the sun was shining, but that it was not very hot. A soft, cool breeze blowing. I am no longer sure. As I am no longer sure what it was like when I first saw the beach that morning. The sea, the sun, the other people: a collage of vaguely recollected, vaguely re-created, perhaps wishful impressions: the not very hot weather, the not entirely bright sun, the not very many people. The soft, cool breeze inserted: perhaps a memory from elsewhere.

In my memory dwell certain words, gestures, acts, incidents, but the surrounding details—the surroundings in general—have faded into a transparent, enveloping aether. For they moved me little, if at all, then. Usually, there, here, elsewhere, I did, do, not notice. The surroundings simply surround. They run up, not quite, to the object of my attention, my affection: a face; a hand; eyes; a phrase; the noise of one single wave breaking on the shore; the heady stench of the rotting seaweed; the taste of the brine on my fingertip; the hot, dry grains of sand—or the cold, damp, pasty sand—on the heels and balls of my feet. And around these sharp impressions there is an aura, an emotion, usually feeble, only momentarily arresting; yet sometimes exalting, overwhelming; and sometimes devastatingly sad. A sadness that will eventually fade away, then weeks, months, years later re-emerge. A sadness coming on all of a sudden, for no identifiable reason, an absorbing sadness . . . and soon I am imagining what was, what might have been, what will or might be. Without knowing it, I will have withdrawn from the world, from the present, every chance perception of the world's particulars thereafter rushing me from myself back to that desperately yearned-for Other, to that impossible, unattainable Otherness, as if a unifying wholeness had been created anew . . .

> I often saw her living (but who would believe me?)
> in the clear water, in the green grass,
> in the trunk of a beech-tree, in a white cloud . . .

until, like Petrarch's, my perceptions again convey only the brute facts they have seized. The clear water: the clear water. The green grass: the green grass. The trunk of the beech-tree—hard to the caressing hand. The white cloud—mere whiteness, mere cloudness, to adoring eyes. The unifying wholeness dissipates and the veritable presence remaining is that of a painful, permanent absence.

> . . . a dead stone on a stone alive,
> resembling a man thinking, weeping and writing . . .

While waiting for the hour to elapse, Ann, Joan and I tried building a sand castle. In the trunk of the car we had found a pail and a spade; in the motel: spoons, cups, and bowls. The tide was still coming in; our high walls rose bucketful by bucketful, handful by handful; we dug a moat around the ramparts, then a canal leading up from the sea. The water surged up the canal, filled the moat; most of the water flowed back to the sea. I suggested: *Let's dig the trench deeper.* Ann: *Let's dam up the canal when the water has filled the moat.*

We dug the trench deeper, but by the time we were patting down the walls, smoothing them out, the water had stopped filling up the moat as completely as before. With each new wave, the water flowed only halfway around. Once surging past our bare feet, now the water touched out toes, receded. The tide was turning. My mother would say: *Sometimes the tide turns in life,* and I can still hear her voice—calm when she said such words—over the roar of the breakers.

We stood there waiting for a powerful wave, a wave more powerful than the others. It wouldn't come. In the moat the water seeped downwards, out of sight, filtering away through the sand. *We'll have to build a new castle,* I said. *Let's find a place where the waves will reach us always.* Reach us always. I tried to imagine a place where the waves would reach us always. Where the motion of things wore down no thing. A place the very essence of which was perpetual motion. No death. My sand castle at the edge of a boundless, benevolent ocean. The turrets rising high above the lapping water. My tiny colored flags mounted on the turrets. Puffs of wind: the flags stirring. The water flowing gently into the moat; gently out.

Then, in my imagination, a mighty wave arose from the placid surface, roared in, shattering the ramparts, leaving a vast, desolate ocean in its wake.

Ann and Joan had long since given up building our castle. They were wading near the shore, looking for shells, starfish, driftwood, washed-up refuse, *bottles with a message inside—do you think we'll find one?* I myself waded (forgetting to run) into the water. In a moment, bracing myself against the cold, I dove headlong into the waves, swam out. It was not easy. Incessantly I strained against their relentless might, struggling to make progress, kicking my feet furiously, rhythmically knifing my arms into the water, pulling hard with my cupped hands. Finally, my arms and shoulders weary, I plunged beneath the crests, opened my eyes, peered into the thick, liquid opaqueness. Saw nothing. Felt a burning. My mother: *Saltwater burns.* Resurfacing, I treaded water for a while, rubbing my eyes with my right hand, then gazed back at the beach.

I suddenly had the disorienting impression that I was merely engaged in an activity. It no longer mattered that it was swimming or treading water. Distinguishing qualities between human endeavors had vanished. I might have been mowing the lawn, back home. I might have been stomping on the silverfish, back in the motel. The separation—but how? but when?—had occurred. I was already elsewhere, abstracted from the dense, enveloping present . . . yet still a part of that present. I was now outside myself, watching myself. Watching myself engaged in an activity, in the world. Watching myself moving, in the world. Watching myself going through the motions, in the world. In the world: in the sea, in the breeze, in the sunlight. In the world: at Seaside. A world inserted in a present doubled over, folded over; or perhaps a present in two parallel parts. For my body now seemed distinct from my mind. For my eye seemed an organ of my body and also the window of my mind. I observed myself moving about in the sea, my head bobbing up and down, my legs and arms rhythmically undulating, while my thoughts were pervaded by the notion, neither despairing nor consoling, that all endeavors, however noble or base, can ultimately be summed up as insignificant wrigglings on the vast empty sea of the universe.

I am wriggling like a water bug on its back.

This vivid hallucination, at once cruel and amusing, revived my dormant fears. After treading water for a while, I had indeed been attempting to float on my back, while tossing to and fro on the waves. I now let my legs dangle down, righting myself. The mortal, barely perceptible dangers reappeared in all their potentialities. I observed, in my imagination, as objectively and as acutely as I could, the dangers. I was afraid. No, I was not really afraid; not very afraid; not too afraid. The jellyfish. The lobsters. The octopuses. The piranahs. *But don't piranahs live in the Amazon?* The entire world reappeared, as if attached to and growing out from these imagined maritime entities. At first somewhat distant, it gradually closed in, enveloped, infiltrated: all the way up to my skin, my chin; all the way into my mouth. I tasted the briny water, spit it out. There is no escaping from the world.

At other times I had had and would have again similar sensations. Once, when very young, while I was being threatened in Beaverdale Park by a high-school hood with a switchblade. The blade twisting and turning in front of my nose; at that very moment the impression that I was a mere speck in the dense, primeval flux; and that this speck was inseparable from the flux, whatever its will. Another time, when much older, while stranded in a tiny elevator, between floors. It was ten o'clock in the morning; not a soul about in that Parisian apartment building; the alarm bell—*working? Is it ringing in some distant custodian's office?* The stuffiness, the heat, the total darkness. My unsuccessful shouts for help while someone came down the stairs, passed right in front of the elevator door, cursing his own misfortune, rushing off to work. The long, dark silence enveloping me until, inexplicably, the elevator started going down again. The doors opened. I found myself in the basement. I bolted up the emergency stairs, pushed open a fire door, pushed a button which opened a second door, stepped out into the bright sunlight, into the hustle and bustle. I immediately became an anonymous passerby to whom, as far as anyone could tell, nothing out of the ordinary had happened. I desired to stop a fellow pedestrian and explain, but, inevitably, continued on my way. Indeed, it was with relief that I found it was possible to insert myself into the rushing stream, to let myself be carried along by the momentum of the crowd, to head with hundreds of indifferent people down into the Métro. Such is my desire, felt so often: to blend into the masses and disappear.

As with the switchblade, as with the elevator, I was retrospectively surprised that I had remained more or less calm, rational, despite my fears. *The jellyfish. The lobsters . . .* I appraised the situation and continued treading water. By that age I of course knew there were no . . . *octopuses, piranahs.* I knew the dangers were imaginary, yet at the same time I could not help but imagine them. *Tomorrow I will return,* I thought, *and swim further out. Swim further out?* I treaded water, hovering above the bottom of the sea, wavering between possibilities. Eventually I decided to swim back to the beach.

I foresaw myself—several yards away—rising out of the shallow water, walking over then trodding through the increasingly heavy sand, towards safety. I imagined myself speaking to my parents, who were still lying out on their towels. I thought: *I must hide my fears from my parents.* I imagined my very words. *It's great swimming in the ocean! Thanks for bringing us here!* I rehearsed my words. *It's great! Really, thanks a lot!*

I was still treading water, not too far from the shore.

Did my father swim out my way?

A recurrent image after all these years: my father's head bobbing above the water, his face facing my own. Yet we were not swimming at Seaside that time, but rather in Des Moines, at Northwest Swimming Pool. I was younger than I was at Seaside; my father's hair—slicked down over his forehead; he was smiling at me; a Saturday afternoon; summery sunlight, boisterous shouting, splashing; we had tried to swim laps together, to dive to the bottom: too many people.

We climbed the deep-end ladder—me, first.

My father undid the two badges safety-pinned to his trunks, handed them to the man at the window; we recovered two wire-mesh baskets full of clothes. Then we went off to the locker room.

A roofless locker room: wooden benches, shower nozzles, cement and tile, the sunlight streaming in.

I was a young boy realizing for the first time that he was studying his father's naked body. The short, curly hairs everywhere, especially on the chest; the large, drooping penis, the dangling scrotum, much larger than my own; most curious of all: the scar. I stared at it. My father asked me what I was looking at.

That strange scar.

I pointed.

It's like there's a hole at the end.

I started to touch the scar, but my father drew back slightly. He put his head under the shower nozzle. I stepped back. The water streamed down over his body, drops splashing from his head and shoulders onto my face. I was holding his towel. In a couple of years I too would undergo an appendectomy. It must have been that following summer that we went to Seaside, for I remember suddenly wondering, while drying off on the beach, whether my swimming trunks covered up my scar. I looked down: they did.

The next thing I recall is eating dinner at a restaurant in the center of town. There were windows all around, more or less as they are in French cafés. But what did I eat? Two cheeseburgers, onion rings and a milkshake? A tenderloin, French fries, a salad and apple pie? There are times when I would like to hold on to even these details. So much of my past: already washed back out to the sea.

It was at that restaurant when, for the first time, I saw hippies. The month and year I can calculate: July, 1966. There were no hippies yet in Des Moines; nor would there ever be many. But early that evening, as the sun was setting—had we walked on the beach just before-hand?—, the hippies started gathering in the streets, strolling past the restaurant, strumming guitars, chatting, embracing, wearing ankle-length dresses, patched jeans, beads, badges, beards, flowers in their long tangled hair, a couple slow-dancing and holding up traffic, a mime imitating someone or something, a prophet of doom with a sandwich board—in protest against the Vietnam War? I cannot remember. Joan noticed a young woman, dressed like a Raggedy-Ann doll, handing out helium-filled balloons. *Mom, can I go outside and get one?* she pleaded. Only with my mother's determined *no!* did I realize why she had been so tense while we were waiting to be served. So it was the hippies. Maybe there was something else as well.

I was glad to be able to observe the hippies—from a distance, from an angle, from behind the window pane.

That night, in bed, I listened to the wind rattling the shutters. I imagined silverfish slithering underneath the bed, thought back on my brief swim in the sea—jellyfish, lobsters, octopuses, piranahs—, *I'll try swimming out further tomorrow* I said to myself, remembered the Raggedy-Ann doll holding a fistful of balloons on a string, recalled the faces of the hippies each in turn, wondered what my mother might be thinking in the bedroom next to mine.

She had been inexplicably silent, sullen, perhaps angry at someone (my father?), looking up at none of us in the restaurant, both her hands clenched. Hurriedly we had eaten; my father had paid the bill; we had left. Back to the motel right away; not even a stroll on the board-walk. *We're all tired,* she had said, *let's go to bed. What time are we getting up tomorrow, Mom?* I asked. No answer came. Or was it: *We'll see.*

It was one of those mysterious, interminable nights which I have since come to know so well. One of those profound, quasi-metaphysical nights—a car-door slammed; the distant siren of an ambulance; an odd ray of light reflected onto the ceiling; a neighbor fumbling for his keys; a child crying; or, instead, absolutely no noise at all: a deep, impenetrable silence . . . —, during which I have the impression of not sleeping at all. And yet, upon awakening, I feel, if not exactly rested, then some-how ready to take on life anew. *So I must have slept,* I think. During such nights I practice up for possible or un-avoidable encounters; compose dialogues with persons loved, distrusted or feared; orchestrate unbelievable coincidences; invent elaborate explanations for acts never committed; re-ceive prizes and distinctions; and, once in a while, close my eyes and concentrate, attempting to draft letters, poems, next paragraphs, repeating sentences over and over until they are memorized. Indeed, during one such night, our trip to Seaside spontaneously came to mind, as from time to time the memory had always re-emerged, unexpectedly, painfully. Twenty-six years had passed. I was listening to a humming sound in a hotel room in northern France. L'Hôtel Mémorial! The luminescent red digits of the electronic clock embedded in the television set reminded me constantly of the time: 1:47. 2:15. 3:34. 5:02. That sleepless night oc-curred in April, last April; and when I arose I jotted down a first sentence: *As a child I had heard my mother talk so often about Seaside. . . .*

What she was thinking, in the motel, I found out the next morning, at dawn. Rising, hoping we could walk on the beach or even take a chilly dip in the sea, I found her drinking a cup of coffee and my father packing our things. Not a word was being said; one or two suitcases stood by

the door. *What's wrong?* I asked. In a moment, Ann and
Joan would be crying, inconsolably. A hasty breakfast of
cereal; the cold milk from the cooler; off we drove, not to
Newport or Pacific City—*Why can't we try another
beach? Maybe it'll be better*—, but back to Lewiston.

I no longer recall what happened during the two or
three weeks that followed. We probably ended up taking
more swimming lessons at the Lewiston Country Club.
Perhaps I played golf with my uncle Bob. And could it
also have been during those scorching hot afternoons—
yes, it must have been—that I would sit at a poolside
table, sipping on a Canada Dry, hardly daring to say a
word while my cousin Marcia chatted about *cute boys*
with her two best friends, Brigitte and Priscilla, who were
twin sisters? Priscilla—but was that her name? It was an
old-fashioned name—Priscilla who also said so little dur-
ing those conversations, who seemed shy and a little
intimidated, whom I would never see in Lewiston again—
her family moved away, Marcia reported the next sum-
mer, *I don't even know where to*—, but whom I ran into
seven years later, at the Denver airport, each of us in-
stantly recognizing the other. We had only ten minutes to
talk, her plane was already boarding—ten minutes to get
acquainted, for we had never gotten to know each other;
yet now it seemed we had always known each other—,
and after Priscilla had disappeared into the Boeing and I
had waved, turned away, started wandering around the
terminal again, in and out of boutiques and newspaper
stands, fingering gadgets and souvenirs, picking up maga-
zines, opening them and setting them back in the racks,
I gradually felt invaded by emotions of loneliness and loss.
Priscilla! We had not even exchanged addresses. Still,
during the next few weeks, although I thought about her

often, something kept me from trying to reach her. And yet I could have reached her, if I had really wanted to: she had mentioned the name of her college in California. All I did was daydream. I tried to recall the features of her face. I tried to recall her words, the tone of her voice. I imagined what it would be like to talk to her on the phone. I even found the words I wanted to say. *Why then do you hesitate?* I asked myself. Finally I must—until just now, when I remembered her while writing this—have thought less and less about, then finally forgotten, Priscilla.

In my memory, no real continuity exists between our one day at Seaside, our stay in Lewiston and our trip back to Des Moines. We must have arrived, driven up the driveway, parked, unpacked the car. School must have started. A new school year must have begun. From a certain vantage point I can say: the school years went by, all the years have gone by, have gone rushing by—all the way up to the present. To now. No, to not quite now. To just a moment ago. For just a moment ago, as I was gazing out the window at the autumn leaves, so fragilely suspended on the branches of the trees, it suddenly seemed that all the intervening years since our trip to Seaside had not—second by second, minute by minute, hour by hour—elapsed. As if all those days, weeks, months had not been lived. Oh, of course I just as quickly remembered . . . and then so much came back to mind . . . other summers . . . other springs . . . other winters . . . other falls . . . and yes I had lived . . . and even lived fully at times . . . , but, strangely, while I was gazing at the leaves (most of them motionless, a few trembling, others falling) fading into images of Seaside, even the most significant subsequent events—those so much more crucial than anything that happened during that brief interval of the past—were swept up into, compressed into, a mere flash of time. My life: an instant! *I remember vacationing at Seaside as if it were yesterday,* my mother would say, holding out the box of saltwater taffy.

Nearly everything that happens remains inconclusive. For years thereafter, I did not go swimming in the sea again. I saw the ocean, both oceans: I walked along the docks in Manhattan, strolled along the beach at Cape Cod, flew over the Atlantic on my first trip to Europe; and during the spring break of our sophomore year, Charlie and I roamed around the wharf in Seattle, then a few days later drove down the coast—through Seaside. An intersection, a stoplight; I remember a hardware store a little further down, on the left. I told him about our family trip. Did I secretly hope we would stay? It was the middle of the afternoon. The sun was shining. The light turned green: we drove on, not far, but on.

The waves at Seaside scurry up the beach—in my mind. Scurry back. The sun shines. The wind softly blows. I recall the taffymaker and open up a little shop for him on the boardwalk. He is a kindly old man. Passersby look in at his machine pulling and stretching the candy. A mother buys a box for her children. Someone else wants a box. A brother and sister glide by, on a tandem, over the whitened, salt-eaten wood. The bicycle shop?—it's there too. So is the dress shop. So is our sand castle, indestructible. The tiny flags on the turrets. So is a fourteen-year-old boy, treading water, hovering above the bottom of the sea, wavering between possibilities, a little·farther out then yesterday; but this time he is fearless. The palm of his hand moves gently, but firmly, through the water. Gently, firmly. He is happy in the world as it is. The world is as it should be. He thinks: *The world is as it is.*

Originally from Des Moines, John Taylor left the United States in 1975, studied in Germany, spent a year in Greece, then settled in France, where he still lives. His first collection of short stories, *The Presence of Things Past* (Story Line Press, 1992), evokes his Midwestern childhood. A sequel, *Mysteries of the Body and the Mind,* was published by Story Line in 1998. As a critic, he regularly contributes articles on contemporary French literature to the *Times Literary Supplement* in London and is responsible for the "Books" pages of *France Magazine,* published by the French Embassy in Washington, D.C.

The French painter Sibylle Baltzer-Hasan was born in 1973. In Paris, her work has been exhibited in several group shows and in two important individual shows. She currently lives and works in London.

Cedar Hill Publications

3722 Hwy. 8 West
Mena, Arkansas 71953

THE WORLD AS IT IS—John Taylor
$10—Prose
ISBN: 1-891812-04-1

AMNESIA TANGO—Alan Britt
$10—Poetry
ISBN: 1-891812-14-9

7th CIRCLE—Maggie Jaffe
$10—Poetry
ISBN: 1-891812-07-6

THE BOOK OF ALLEGORY—Michael McIrvin
$10—Poetry
ISBN: 1-891812-03-3

"EDEN, OVER . . ."—Tim Scannell
$5—Poetry
ISBN: 1-891812-01-7

PIECES OF EIGHT: A Women's Anthology of Verse
$10—Poetry
ISBN: 1-891812-02-5

THE TERRIBLE WILDERNESS OF SELF—Leonard Cirino
$10—Poetry
ISBN: 1-891812-00-9

Forthcoming:

JAM: Cedar Hill Anthology Series
$8—Poetry
ISBN: 1-891812-05-X

DANCE: Cedar Hill Anthology Series
$8—Poetry

PROVERBS FOR THE INITIATED—Kenn Mitchell
$10—Poetry

DARK ROSE DIALOGUE—Christopher Presfield
$4—Poetry

Available from:
Amazon.com
http://www.amazon.com/

888. 422. 0320 X4144